Mother's 5-Minute Mornings with God

SHORT, COLORFUL YET MEANINGFUL 90-DAY DAILY DEVOTIONAL BEFORE THE DAY STARTS

ANCHORED GRACE PUBLISHING

A Gift for You

Thank you for choosing this devotional.

To support your journey of faith, we created a special gift bundle for our readers.

Inside the Anchored Grace Reader Gift Bundle, you will receive:

A free digital devotional

Printable prayer journal pages

Scripture reflection cards

Bonus devotionals for different seasons of life

Daily encouragement from Anchored Grace

Simply scan the QR code below or visit the link to receive your free bundle.

devo.anchoredgraces.com/mothergift

Scan the QR code with your phone camera or type the link into your browser.

We pray these resources continue to encourage your heart each day.

EMBRACING GRACE

"And my God will meet all your needs according to the riches of his glory in Christ Jesus."

PHILIPPIANS 4:19

DEVOTION

Embracing grace means recognizing that you are deserving of kindness, especially from yourself, as you navigate the beautiful, chaotic journey of motherhood.

REFLECTION

What does it mean for you to fully embrace grace in your daily life as a mother and a woman? How can letting go of perfection open your heart to the beauty of God's love?

____

____

____

____

PRAYER

Dear Lord, help me to embrace Your grace in my life. Let me feel Your presence in every moment, allowing Your love to transform my heart and guide my steps each day.

Embracing grace means recognizing that our worth is not based on our performance, but on God's unwavering love.

THE POWER OF PRAYER

"Do not be anxious about anything, but in every situation, by prayer and petition, with thanksgiving, present your requests to God. 7 And the peace of God, which transcends all understanding, will guard your hearts and your minds in Christ Jesus."

PHILIPPIANS 4:6-7

DEVOTION

Prayer is not just a ritual; it is a powerful conversation that nurtures our hearts and reminds us of our strength in Christ.

REFLECTION

What does your heart long to bring before God in prayer today? In what areas of your life can you invite His presence and guidance more fully?

____

____

____

____

PRAYER

Dear Lord, thank you for the gift of prayer that connects us to You. Help us to carve out quiet moments to seek Your will and wisdom in our busy lives, drawing us closer to You each day.

Prayer is the bridge that connects our hearts to God's promises.

FINDING JOY IN CHAOS

"A cheerful heart is good medicine, but a broken spirit saps a person's strength."

PROVERBS 17:22

DEVOTION

No matter how turbulent life can get, it's in these fleeting, joyful moments that we often find more strength and resilience than we realize. Embrace chaos as an opportunity to discover laughter and love amidst the noise.

REFLECTION

What brings you joy amidst the busyness and chaos of your daily life? Can you think of a moment today when you felt a glimmer of happiness, even in the midst of a challenging situation?

____

____

____

____

PRAYER

Dear God, thank you for the simple joys that often go unnoticed in our chaotic lives. Help me to find and cherish these moments, reminding me of your love and presence even in the storm.

**Joy often blooms
in the unlikeliest of places.**

NAVIGATING MOM GUILT

"She is clothed with strength and dignity; she can laugh at the days to come."

PROVERBS 31:25

DEVOTION

Embrace the beautiful mess of motherhood and find joy in the imperfect moments, knowing you are doing your best.

REFLECTION

What moments have you felt that familiar twinge of guilt as a mom? How did those feelings impact your day, your choices, or even your perspective on parenting?

____

____

____

____

PRAYER

Dear God, help us embrace the unique challenges of motherhood without the weight of guilt. May we find grace in our imperfections and peace in our daily choices. Amen.

Motherhood is not about perfection; it's about presence and love.

EVERYDAY MIRACLES

"Blessed are those who have not seen and yet have believed."

JOHN 20:29

DEVOTION

Even in the tasks that seem mundane, there is beauty and wonder waiting to be discovered in the daily moments of motherhood.

REFLECTION

What small moments in your day feel like gifts, reminding you of the miracles around you? How can you cultivate awareness for these everyday blessings?

____

____

____

____

PRAYER

Dear Lord, thank you for the little wonders that fill our lives with joy. Help us to see and appreciate each miracle, no matter how small, that you place before us every day.

Everyday miracles are the whispers of grace we often overlook, waiting to be noticed and embraced.

SURRENDERING CONTROL

"So do not fear, for I am with you; do not be dismayed, for I am your God; I will strengthen you and help you; I will uphold you with my righteous right hand."

ISAIAH 41:10

DEVOTION

Sometimes, true strength lies not in holding tightly to every detail, but in releasing control and trusting God with our journey.

REFLECTION

What are the areas of your life where you struggle to let go and trust God's plan instead of trying to control the outcome?

____

____

____

____

PRAYER

Dear God, help me to release my need for control and to trust in Your wisdom and timing. Fill my heart with peace as I learn to surrender my worries into Your caring hands.

True freedom comes when we release our grip and allow life to unfold in its own beautiful way.

FELLOWSHIP WITH OTHER MOTHERS

"Two are better than one, because they have a good reward for their toil. For if they fall, one will lift up his fellow; but woe to him who is alone when he falls and has not another to lift him up."

ECCLESIASTES 4:9-10

DEVOTION

In the journey of motherhood, building fellowship with other mothers can provide the encouragement and strength we need to navigate our days.

REFLECTION

What joys and challenges do you share with other mothers that deepen your connections and understanding of each other's journeys?

____

____

____

____

PRAYER

Dear God, thank you for the gift of community and the bonds we share as mothers. Help us to seek one another, share our stories, and uplift each other with love and support.

In the company of mothers, we find strength in vulnerability and joy in shared experiences.

One Week Together

You've just completed your first week of devotionals.

If these reflections have brought peace or encouragement into your day, would you consider sharing a short Amazon review?

devo.anchoredgraces.com/mother

Your words help other women discover devotionals that may support them on their own faith journey.

Thank you for spending these moments in reflection.

PARENTING WITH PURPOSE

"Train up a child in the way he should go; even
when he is old he will not depart from it."

PROVERBS 22:6

DEVOTION

Parenting with purpose means embracing the
everyday moments that nurture your child's
heart and spirit.

REFLECTION

What are the core values you hope to instill in your children, and how can you embody those values in your everyday actions?

____

____

____

____

PRAYER

Dear God, thank you for the gift of motherhood. Help me to parent with intention and love, reflecting Your grace in my decisions and actions. Guide me to nurture my children with purpose in every moment we share.

Parenting is not just about raising children; it's about shaping the future through the values we teach today.

THE GIFT OF REST

"Come to me, all you who are weary and burdened, and I will give you rest."

MATTHEW 11:28

DEVOTION

In the chaos of motherhood and life's commitments, remember that taking time to rest is not merely a luxury; it's a necessary act of self-care that enriches your spirit and enhances your presence for those you love.

REFLECTION

What does taking time for rest mean to you as a
mother, and how can you create space for it in
your daily life?

____

____

____

____

PRAYER

Dear Heavenly Father, thank you for the gift of
rest that you provide us. Help us to embrace
moments of stillness amid the chaos of
motherhood, allowing our spirits to be renewed
and our minds to be refreshed.

**Rest is not a luxury; it is a necessity
for our souls to flourish.**

LOVING YOURSELF

"I praise you because I am fearfully and wonderfully made; your works are wonderful, I know that full well."

PSALM 139:14

DEVOTION

Loving yourself is not just an indulgence; it is an essential practice that empowers you to love and serve others more fully.

REFLECTION

What does loving yourself mean to you, and in what ways can you honor your needs and feelings today? Consider how you might treat yourself with the same kindness and grace you offer to others.

____

____

____

____

PRAYER

Dear God, help me to embrace my worth and nurture my spirit. May I find joy in who I am and see my value through Your eyes. Amen.

Embracing self-love is not selfish; it is a sacred act of honoring the beautiful creation that you are.

CULTIVATING PATIENCE

"Be completely humble and gentle; be patient, bearing with one another in love."

EPHESIANS 4:2

DEVOTION

In the midst of life's chaos, cultivating patience not only nurtures our relationships but also fosters a deeper sense of peace within ourselves.

REFLECTION

What situations in your life challenge your patience the most, and how can you respond to them with grace and understanding? Consider what steps you can take to cultivate a more patient heart in these moments.

____

____

____

____

PRAYER

Dear God, thank You for the beautiful journey of motherhood and the lessons it brings. Help me to embrace each day with patience, trusting in Your timing and love. Amen.

Patience is not the ability to wait, but the ability to keep a good attitude while waiting.

FROM WORRY TO WORSHIP

"Cast all your anxiety on him because he cares for you."

1 PETER 5:7

DEVOTION

In quiet moments of gratitude and worship, we discover that our worries can be transformed into a deeper trust in God's care.

REFLECTION

What worries are weighing on your heart today, and how might you invite God into those concerns to transform them into moments of worship?

____

____

____

____

PRAYER

Lord, help me to lay my worries at Your feet and replace them with praise. Remind me that in every moment of uncertainty, Your presence is a source of peace and strength.

Where worry seeks to steal my joy, worship invites me into His presence.

CREATING A FAITH-CENTERED HOME

"My people will abide in a peaceful habitation, in secure dwellings, and in quiet resting places."

ISAIAH 32:18

DEVOTION

A faith-centered home is not about eliminating chaos, but about inviting peace into the midst of it.

REFLECTION

What are some specific ways you can infuse your home with faith today, creating an environment where love and spirituality flourish for you and your family? Reflect on small, intentional actions that can make a difference.

____

____

____

____

PRAYER

Dear God, thank you for the gift of family and the opportunity to nurture a faith-centered home. Help me to be a light in my space, guiding my loved ones closer to Your heart each day.

Home is where our faith takes root, growing and blooming in the warmth of love and understanding.

THE ROLE OF FORGIVENESS

"Be kind and compassionate to one another, forgiving each other, just as in Christ God forgave you."

EPHESIANS 4:32

DEVOTION

Forgiveness is not just a gift we offer others; it's a liberating act for our own hearts, allowing us to heal and embrace joy once again.

REFLECTION

What burdens are you carrying that could be lifted through the power of forgiveness?

____

____

____

____

PRAYER

Heavenly Father, help me to let go of the hurts that weigh heavy on my heart. Teach me the beauty of forgiving others as You have forgiven me, filling my spirit with peace and grace.

Forgiveness is a gift we give ourselves—releasing the shackles of resentment and welcoming the freedom of healing.

BALANCING WORK AND FAMILY

"Her children rise up and call her blessed; her husband also, and he praises her."

PROVERBS 31:28

DEVOTION

Finding balance in work and family often requires intentional choices, leading to the realization that carving out quality time reaps profound rewards in relationships and personal joy.

REFLECTION

What small adjustments can you make in your daily routine to feel more present with your family while still pursuing your career goals?

____

____

____

____

PRAYER

Heavenly Father, help me find peace in the balance of work and family. Grant me the wisdom to prioritize what truly matters and the strength to embrace both my professional ambitions and my cherished role as a mother.

Balance is not something you find; it's something you create.

DAILY DEVOTIONS

Trust in the Lord with all your heart and lean not on your own understanding; in all your ways submit to Him, and He will make your paths straight."

PROVERBS 3:5-6

DEVOTION

Let go of the burdens you carry and remember to trust God with all parts of your life, for He walks beside you, guiding your steps even in the busiest of seasons.

REFLECTION

What is one small way you can invite God into your daily routine today? How might that shift your perspective or actions?

____

____

____

____

PRAYER

Dear Lord, thank You for being present in our everyday lives. Help me to find joy in the small moments and to feel Your guidance as I navigate my day.

Even in the midst of chaos, God can bring clarity and peace.

THE BLESSING OF MOTHERHOOD

"She is clothed with strength and dignity; she can laugh at the days to come. She opens her mouth with wisdom, and the teaching of kindness is on her tongue."

PROVERBS 31:25-26

DEVOTION

The true blessing of motherhood lies not only in the love we give but in the legacy of compassion and strength we nurture within our children.

REFLECTION

What moments in your motherhood journey have filled your heart with gratitude and joy? How have these experiences shaped your understanding of love and sacrifice?

____

____

____

____

PRAYER

Dear Lord, thank you for the gift of motherhood. Help me to embrace each moment with grace, capturing the blessings woven into the fabric of my daily life.

Motherhood is not just a role; it's an ever-evolving journey of love, resilience, and grace.

TRUSTING GOD'S TIMING

"Wait for the Lord; be strong and take heart and wait for the Lord."

PSALM 27:14

DEVOTION

Trusting God's timing can reveal blessings that far surpass our own plans.

REFLECTION

What areas of your life have you found yourself waiting on God lately, and how can you embrace the wait as a part of His perfect plan for you?

____

____

____

____

PRAYER

Dear Lord, help me to trust in Your timing, knowing that You have a purpose for every season of my life. Teach me to find peace and joy as I wait on You.

Sometimes, waiting is the most powerful act of faith we can offer.

BUILDING RESILIENCE

"…but those who hope in the Lord
will renew their strength.
They will soar on wings like eagles;
they will run and not grow weary,
they will walk and not be faint."

ISAIAH 40:31

DEVOTION

Embrace the beauty of resilience; it thrives not
only in your strength but also in your willingness
to share your journey with others.

REFLECTION

What challenges have you faced recently that tested your resilience, and how did you respond to them? Reflect on the strength you might have discovered within yourself during those times.

____

____

____

____

PRAYER

Dear God, help me to embrace the challenges I face with grace and courage. Fill my heart with strength and remind me that every obstacle is an opportunity to grow.

Resilience is not just about bouncing back; it's about thriving amidst uncertainty and finding strength in vulnerability.

FINDING COMMUNITY

"As iron sharpens iron, so one person sharpens another."

PROVERBS 27:17

DEVOTION

Embrace the courage to reach out; in vulnerability, you will discover deep connections that enrich your life.

REFLECTION

What does community look like in your life right now, and how can you invite deeper connections into it?

____

____

____

____

PRAYER

Dear Lord, thank You for the gift of community. Help me to open my heart to those around me, fostering connections that uplift and support. Guide my steps as I seek to create meaningful relationships.

Community isn't just about being together; it's about finding strength in our shared journeys.

TEACHING FAITH TO OUR CHILDREN

"But as for me and my household, we will serve the Lord."

JOSHUA 24:15

DEVOTION

In nurturing our children's faith, we create spaces for open dialogue, allowing them to see how our beliefs shape our choices and actions.

REFLECTION

What are some ways you can weave faith into your daily conversations and activities with your children, making it a natural part of their lives?

____

____

____

____

PRAYER

Dear Lord, may I be a guiding light for my children, nurturing their hearts with the warmth of Your love and teaching them to trust in Your goodness. Help me to share my faith in a gentle and meaningful way.

Faith is not just taught; it is caught in the everyday moments we share.

Three Weeks of Reflection

You've now spent several weeks walking through these devotionals.

If this book has encouraged your heart, a brief Amazon review helps other women find the same encouragement.

devo.anchoredgraces.com/mother

Your experience may guide someone else toward the hope they are searching for.

Thank you for being here.

NAVIGATING SEASONS OF CHANGE

"See, I am doing a new thing! Now it springs up;
do you not perceive it?"

ISAIAH 43:19

DEVOTION

Embracing change can foster growth that
prepares us for the beautiful chapters yet to
come.

REFLECTION

What changes are you currently navigating in your life, and how can you embrace them with grace and faith?

____

____

____

____

PRAYER

Dear God, help me to see the beauty in every season of change I face. Grant me the courage to embrace transformation and the wisdom to find joy in the journey.

Change is not only a part of life; it is the pathway to growth and renewal.

HOPE IN DIFFICULT TIMES

"For I know the plans I have for you," declares the Lord, "plans to prosper you and not to harm you, plans to give you hope and a future."

JEREMIAH 29:11

DEVOTION

In difficult times, remember that God often uses our hardships to pave the way for new beginnings and unexpected blessings.

REFLECTION

What difficult situation are you currently facing, and how can you invite God into that space to bring you hope and comfort?

____

____

____

____

PRAYER

Heavenly Father, as I navigate these challenging times, help me to rest in Your promises and find peace in Your presence. Grant me the strength to hold onto hope, even when the path seems unclear.

Hope isn't just a feeling; it's a choice to trust that God has a plan, even in the uncertainty.

CREATIVE CONNECTIONS

"Therefore encourage one another and build each other up, just as in fact you are doing."

1 THESSALONIANS 5:11

DEVOTION

The relationships we cultivate can nourish our spirits and remind us that we're never alone in this journey.

REFLECTION

What creative connections have you made in your life that have enriched your journey as a mother and nurtured your spirit? How can you further cultivate those connections?

____

____

____

____

PRAYER

Dear God, thank You for the beautiful connections in our lives. Help us to see the miracles in everyday moments and to strengthen the bonds that uplift and inspire us.

Connection is not just a bond; it's the bridge to the soul.

THE BLESSINGS OF DISCIPLINE

"Whoever loves discipline loves knowledge, but whoever hates correction is stupid."

PROVERBS 12:1

DEVOTION

Discipline may feel restrictive at times, but it ultimately paves the way for deeper knowledge, personal growth, and a more harmonious family life.

REFLECTION

What areas of your life could use a bit more discipline, and how might embracing this blessing lead to greater peace and fulfillment for you and your family?

____

____

____

____

PRAYER

Dear God, thank You for the gift of discipline in our lives. Help us to embrace it with grace and to see the beauty it can bring to our daily routines and relationships. Fill our hearts with strength as we strive for balance and growth.

Discipline is the bridge between goals and accomplishments, guiding us to the life we desire.

SPIRITUAL WARFARE

"Finally, be strong in the Lord and in his mighty power. Put on the full armor of God so that you can take your stand against the devil's schemes."

EPHESIANS 6:10-11

DEVOTION

In the daily battles we encounter, we must remember to equip ourselves with faith and rely on God's strength, knowing that we are never alone in our struggles.

REFLECTION

What battles are you facing in your daily life,
and how might God's strength help you
overcome them?

____

____

____

____

PRAYER

Dear God, thank you for being with us in our
struggles. Help us to recognize your power and
love as we navigate the challenges of our lives.
Equip us with faith and courage to stand firm in
your truth.

**In the midst of spiritual warfare,
remember that your strength lies
not in your abilities but in your
relationship with God.**

FACING ANXIETY WITH FAITH

"Peace I leave with you; my peace I give you. I do not give to you as the world gives. Do not let your hearts be troubled and do not be afraid."

JOHN 14:27

DEVOTION

Even when it feels like the world is pressing in, choosing to let God's peace fill your heart can transform anxiety into a moment of divine rest.

REFLECTION

What anxieties are currently weighing on your heart, and how might you invite God into those moments of uncertainty?

____

____

____

____

PRAYER

Dear Lord, as I navigate these waves of anxiety, I ask for Your peace to wash over me. Help me to trust in Your plan and lean on Your strength in times of worry.

Faith is the bridge between where I am and where I want to be.

INVESTING TIME IN RELATIONSHIPS

"A friend loves at all times, and a brother is born for a time of adversity."

PROVERBS 17:17

DEVOTION

Prioritize and cherish your relationships, for they are the anchors that keep you steady in life's storms.

REFLECTION

What relationships in your life need more of your time and attention right now? How can you intentionally invest in nurturing those connections?

____

____

____

____

PRAYER

Dear Lord, thank you for the gift of relationships. Help me to be present and intentional, creating time to nurture the bonds that enrich my life and the lives of those I love.

Relationships flourish when we invest not just time, but our hearts.

GOD'S LOVE IN ACTION

"Though the mountains be shaken and the hills be removed, yet my unfailing love for you will not be shaken."

ISAIAH 54:10

DEVOTION

Even when life feels overwhelming, God's love is revealed in the moments of connection with our loved ones.

REFLECTION

What does God's love in action look like in your everyday life? How can you intentionally share that love with your family and those around you?

____

____

____

____

PRAYER

Dear God, help me to recognize and embrace Your love in my daily life. May I reflect that love to my family and friends, becoming a vessel of Your grace and kindness. Thank you for constantly guiding me on this journey.

God's love is not just a feeling; it's a force that moves us to act.

THE INFLUENCE OF A MOTHER'S LOVE

"As a mother comforts her child, so will I comfort you; and you will be comforted over Jerusalem."

ISAIAH 66:13

DEVOTION

The influence of a mother's love can create a safe haven during life's storms, reflecting the warmth and strength that can guide our children through their struggles.

REFLECTION

What are some ways you can actively show your children the depth of your love for them today, even in the smallest moments? How might those gestures shape their understanding of love and connection?

____

____

____

____

PRAYER

Dear God, thank you for the gift of motherhood. Please help us to reflect Your love in our daily lives, teaching our children grace, compassion, and strength through our actions. Amen.

A mother's love is the quiet strength that builds a child's foundation.

EMBRACING CHANGE

"Therefore we do not lose heart. Though outwardly we are wasting away, yet inwardly we are being renewed day by day."

2 CORINTHIANS 4:16

DEVOTION

Change is not the end of who you were; it is the beginning of who you are becoming.

REFLECTION

What changes are occurring in your life right now, and how can you open your heart to embrace them as part of your personal journey? How might these changes be guiding you toward growth and new opportunities?

____

____

____

____

PRAYER

Dear God, help us to see the beauty in the changes of our lives. May we find strength and grace to navigate transitions, trusting that they lead us closer to Your purpose for us.

In every change lies the seed of growth; embrace it and let it blossom.

LEADING FAMILY WORSHIP

"Behold, I and the children God has given me."

HEBREWS 2:13

DEVOTION

The act of leading family worship can forge deeper connections among family members and nurture everyone's faith journey, reminding us that spirituality is a shared experience.

REFLECTION

What are the ways you can create a space for worship in your home that feels inviting and genuine for your family?

____

____

____

____

PRAYER

Dear God, thank You for the gift of family and the opportunity to lead them in worship. Help me to create a warm environment where Your presence is felt, and our hearts are aligned with Yours. Amen.

Worshiping together weaves love and connection into the fabric of our family life.

PRAYER STRATEGIES FOR CHILDREN

"Children are a heritage from the Lord, offspring a reward from Him."

PSALM 127:3

DEVOTION

When facing your children's struggles, remember that prayer is not merely a tool but a partnership with God, inviting Him into their journey and offering them your unwavering support.

REFLECTION

What specific concerns or challenges are you facing with your children today that could be eased through prayer? How can you invite God into these moments to guide you and them on this journey?

____

____

____

____

PRAYER

Heavenly Father, thank you for the precious gift of children. Help me to come to You in prayer, seeking Your wisdom and guidance as I raise them in love and faith.

Prayer is the bridge that connects our hearts to God's promises for our children.

THE ROLE OF GRANDMOTHERS

"Children's children are a crown to the aged, and parents are the pride of their children."

PROVERBS 17:6

DEVOTION

As a woman in your 40s and beyond, cherish the time you spend with your grandchildren, for in these moments, you are sowing seeds of love and wisdom that will bloom for generations to come.

REFLECTION

What gifts or lessons have your own grandmothers imparted to you that continue to shape your life today? How can you embrace those qualities and pass them on to your children and grandchildren?

____

____

____

____

PRAYER

Dear God, thank You for the blessing of grandmothers in our lives. Help us to honor their wisdom and love, carrying their legacy forward in our own families.

Grandmothers are the keepers of family stories, weaving a tapestry of love and legacy that spans generations.

MENTORSHIP IN MOTHERHOOD

"One generation shall commend your works to another, and shall declare your mighty acts."

PSALM 145:4

DEVOTION

In motherhood, every moment spent together is an opportunity to pass on strength and guidance to the next generation.

REFLECTION

What does mentorship in motherhood look like for you, and how can you embrace those who look up to you while seeking guidance from those you admire?

____

____

____

____

PRAYER

Dear Lord, thank You for the wonderful gift of motherhood. Help me to be a wise mentor to my children and those around me, and guide my heart as I seek to learn from others in this beautiful journey.

Every mother is both a student and a teacher, learning from her own experience while sharing wisdom with others.

BALANCING TECHNOLOGY AND FAITH

"Finally, brothers and sisters, whatever is true, whatever is noble, whatever is right, whatever is pure, whatever is lovely, whatever is admirable—if anything is excellent or praiseworthy—think about such things."

PHILIPPIANS 4:8

DEVOTION

We must actively curate what we allow into our minds and hearts, recognizing that our value is found not in likes but in the love we give and receive around us.

REFLECTION

What does your daily technology use reveal about your priorities in faith and family?

____

____

____

____

PRAYER

Dear God, help me to find balance in my daily life, embracing the blessings of technology while nurturing my relationship with You and my family. May I be intentional in how I use my time and tools, seeking Your wisdom in all things.

In the noise of technology, may I find the stillness of Your presence.

TRUSTING GOD WITH OUR DREAMS

"Delight yourself in the Lord, and He will give you the desires of your heart."

PSALM 37:4

DEVOTION

Trusting God with our dreams means releasing control and embracing the journey ahead, knowing He aligns our desires with His perfect will.

REFLECTION

What dreams have you placed in God's hands, and how can you practice trust in His timing today?

____

____

____

____

PRAYER

Dear God, help me to surrender my dreams to You, trusting that You know what is best for my life. Fill my heart with peace as I navigate the journey ahead, knowing You are guiding my steps.

Trusting God with our dreams allows us to embrace possibilities we never could have imagined.

FINDING COMFORT IN GOD'S WORD

"My comfort in my suffering is this: Your promise preserves my life."

PSALM 119:50

DEVOTION

In the ebb and flow of life, lean into God's promises; they are your anchor in times of distress.

REFLECTION

What words or verses in the Bible have provided you comfort in times of distress? How can you carve out moments in your busy day to reflect on these truths?

____

____

____

____

PRAYER

Heavenly Father, thank you for your Word, which brings light to our darkest days. Help me to lean on your promises and find solace in the scriptures, knowing that your love surrounds me always.

God's Word is a soothing balm for the weary soul.

THE ART OF LISTENING

"To answer before listening—that is folly and shame."

PROVERBS 18:13

DEVOTION

Listening is not merely hearing; it's a profound act of love that can transform relationships.

REFLECTION

What are the moments in your daily life when you find it challenging to truly listen to others, and how might this affect your relationships?

____

____

____

____

PRAYER

Dear God, help me to open my heart and ears to those around me. May I find the grace to listen deeply and respond with love and understanding.

Listening is not just hearing the words; it's embracing the heart behind them.

CULTIVATING A GENEROUS SPIRIT

"A generous person will prosper; whoever refreshes others will be refreshed."

PROVERBS 11:25

DEVOTION

In the chaos of life, a simple act of generosity can transform our perspective and foster connections that bring joy to both ourselves and others.

REFLECTION

What does it mean for you to cultivate a generous spirit in your daily life, both within your family and in your community?

____

____

____

____

PRAYER

Dear God, open my heart to the beauty of generosity. Help me to see the needs of those around me and give me the courage to share my time, love, and resources generously.

Generosity is not just what we give, but how we open our hearts to connect with others.

OVERCOMING COMPARISON

"Let us not become weary in doing good, for at the proper time we will reap a harvest if we do not give up."

GALATIANS 6:9

DEVOTION

You are uniquely crafted for your journey, and your worth is not defined by anyone else's achievements or highlights.

REFLECTION

What would your life look like if you released the weight of comparison and embraced the unique journey that God has given you? How would you celebrate your own achievements rather than measuring them against others?

____

____

____

____

PRAYER

Dear God, help me to embrace my unique path and see the beauty in my individuality. Grant me the wisdom to appreciate where I am today without comparing it to others. Amen.

Your worth is not defined by others; it is beautifully crafted by the Creator.

MANAGING STRESS IN MOTHERHOOD

"Come to me, all you who are weary and burdened, and I will give you rest."

MATTHEW 11:28-30

DEVOTION

Remember that even amidst the busyness, taking a moment to breathe and seek God's peace can transform your day and nurture your soul.

REFLECTION

What are the specific stressors in your life as a mother that you can surrender to God today? How might you prioritize self-care while also caring for your family?

____

____

____

____

PRAYER

Dear God, thank you for the gift of motherhood. Help me to find peace amidst the chaos and remind me to lean on you for strength.

In the midst of motherhood's demands, remember that taking a moment for yourself is not selfish —it's essential.

MAKING TIME FOR GOD

"Be still, and know that I am God."

PSALM 46:10

DEVOTION

Making time for God is not just a luxury; it is a necessity that nourishes our spirit and guides us through the challenges of motherhood and life.

REFLECTION

What are some ways you can intentionally carve out time in your busy schedule to nurture your relationship with God?

____

____

____

____

PRAYER

Dear God, help us to find moments in our day where we can pause, connect, and deepen our relationship with You. May we be open to the quiet whispers of Your presence in the midst of our daily chaos.

When we make space for God, we invite peace and purpose into our lives.

THE STRENGTH OF VULNERABILITY

"God is our refuge and strength, a very present help in trouble."

PSALM 46:1

DEVOTION

Embrace your vulnerabilities as a source of strength, knowing that sharing your heart can lead to deeper relationships and greater resilience.

REFLECTION

What does it mean for you to embrace vulnerability in your life, and how can it become a source of strength rather than a weakness?

____

____

____

____

PRAYER

Dear Lord, help me to see the beauty in my vulnerability. May I find strength in sharing my heart and experiences, and trust that you walk with me through every challenge. Amen.

True strength lies not in the absence of fear but in the courage to share our authentic selves.

HOLISTIC HEALTH
FOR MOMS

"I can do all things through Christ who strengthens me."

PHILIPPIANS 4:13

DEVOTION

Your health is a vital thread in the fabric of your family's well-being.

REFLECTION

What does holistic health mean to you as a mother, and how can you incorporate nurturing your mind, body, and spirit into your daily routine?

____

____

____

____

PRAYER

Dear God, thank you for the gift of motherhood and the unique way it shapes us. Help me to embrace a holistic approach to my well-being, guiding me to care for myself as I care for my family.

True wellness encompasses not just the body, but also the heart and soul, creating a balanced life.

Halfway Through Our Journey

You are now halfway through this devotional journey.

Many women discover this book through the thoughtful reviews shared by readers like you.

If these pages have supported your faith and daily reflection, would you consider sharing a short review on Amazon?

Your voice may help someone else find encouragement today.

devo.anchoredgraces.com/mother

EXPLORING SPIRITUAL GIFTS

"God has given each of us a gift from His great variety of spiritual gifts. Use them well to serve one another."

1 PETER 4:10

DEVOTION

You are never too old to recognize and embrace the gifts God has placed within you; your talents can bring light and connection to those around you.

REFLECTION

What unique gifts have you been blessed with,
and how can you nurture them to serve your
family and community?

____

____

____

____

PRAYER

Dear God, thank You for the special gifts You
have placed within me. Help me to recognize
and embrace them, so that I may share Your love
and light with others.

**Your gifts are not only for you;
they are meant to enrich the lives
of those around you.**

LIVING OUT
FAITH IN PUBLIC

"I will say of the Lord, 'He is my refuge and my fortress, my God, in whom I trust.'"

PSALM 91:2

DEVOTION

Living out your faith in public starts with showing compassion and understanding to those around you, reminding others of God's love through your actions.

REFLECTION

What does living out your faith in public look like in your daily interactions with family, friends, and even strangers? How can your actions reflect your beliefs in a way that inspires others?

____

____

____

____

PRAYER

Dear Lord, help me to embody your love and grace in all my encounters today. Give me strength to be a light in the lives of those around me, reflecting Your kindness and compassion.

Our faith is best expressed in the love we show to those around us.

THE JOURNEY OF LETTING GO

"Cast your cares on the Lord and He will sustain you; He will never let the righteous be shaken."

PSALM 55:22

DEVOTION

Sometimes, letting go means trusting that we are supported by a strength greater than ourselves, allowing for peace to enter where anxiety once lived.

REFLECTION

What are the things in your life that you are holding onto, and how might your life change if you choose to release them?

____

____

____

____

PRAYER

Dear God, help me to embrace the courage to let go of what I no longer need. May I find peace and strength in the journey ahead, trusting in Your guidance. Amen.

Letting go is not forgetting; it is a sacred act of love that opens space for new beginnings.

CELEBRATING EVERYDAY MOMENTS

"A joyful heart makes a cheerful face, but by sorrow of heart the spirit is crushed."

PROVERBS 15:13

DEVOTION

Embrace the gift of everyday moments; they are the threads that weave joy into the fabric of your life.

REFLECTION

What small moments in your day bring you the most joy, and how can you celebrate them more intentionally?

____

____

____

____

PRAYER

Dear God, thank you for the little blessings that fill our days. Help us to recognize and cherish these moments, finding joy in the ordinary. Amen.

Everyday moments are the threads that weave joy into the fabric of our lives.

FINDING YOUR VOICE

"She opens her mouth with wisdom, and the teaching of kindness is on her tongue."

PROVERBS 31:26

DEVOTION

Finding your voice is a journey that invites you to recognize your worth and share your wisdom boldly with the world.

REFLECTION

What does it mean for you to truly find your voice, and how can you express it more boldly in your daily life? Reflect on moments when you felt empowered to speak up and the impact it had on you and those around you.

———————————————————

———————————————————

———————————————————

———————————————————

PRAYER

Dear God, thank you for the unique voice you have given me. Help me to recognize its worth and to share it with others, speaking truth and love into my world.

Your voice is a powerful tool; it can heal, inspire, and change the world.

EMBRACING SILENCE

"In Your strength, the king rejoices, O Lord, and in Your salvation how greatly he exalts!"

PSALM 21:1

DEVOTION

Amid the chaos of motherhood and the demands of daily life, carving out time for silence is not a luxury but a necessity that can renew and inspire you.

REFLECTION

What does embracing silence look like for you in your busy life as a mother? How can you carve out moments to connect with the quiet within and listen to what your heart truly needs?

____

____

____

____

PRAYER

Dear God, thank You for the gift of silence amidst the chaos of everyday life. Help me to embrace these quiet moments, to find strength and clarity in Your presence, and to listen to the gentle whispers of my soul.

In silence, we discover the voice of our hearts, guiding us towards true peace.

DEVELOPING A
BIBLE STUDY HABIT

"...and if you look for it as for silver
and search for it as for hidden treasure, then
you will understand the fear of the Lord
and find the knowledge of God."

PROVERBS 2:4-5

DEVOTION

Investing small pockets of time into Bible study
can lead to profound clarity and wisdom in your
life.

REFLECTION

What challenges or distractions do you face that make it difficult to set aside time for Bible study, and how might you overcome them today?

____

____

____

____

PRAYER

Dear Lord, thank you for the gift of your Word. Help me cultivate a consistent habit of studying the Bible, filling my heart and mind with truth and wisdom each day.

Every moment spent in God's Word is an investment in your spirit, nurturing your soul to bloom where it is planted.

CONNECTING THROUGH STORYTELLING

"We will not hide them from their descendants; we will tell the next generation the praiseworthy deeds of the Lord, his power, and the wonders he has done."

PSALM 78:4

DEVOTION

Stories have the power to connect generations, nurturing bonds and building understanding through shared experiences.

REFLECTION

What stories have shaped your life, and how can sharing them create deeper connections with those you love?

____

____

____

____

PRAYER

Dear God, thank you for the unique stories you weave into our lives. Help us to embrace our narratives and share them with love, fostering connection and understanding with those around us.

Every story we tell is a bridge we build, linking our hearts to others.

COPING WITH LOSS

"The Lord is close to the brokenhearted and saves those who are crushed in spirit."

PSALM 34:18

DEVOTION

In times of loss, remember that your love can keep the memory of those you've lost alive, nurturing both your heart and the hearts of those around you.

REFLECTION

What memories or feelings surface for you when
you think about your loss, and how can you
allow yourself to honor those emotions today?

____

____

____

____

PRAYER

Dear God, as I navigate this journey of loss, help
me find comfort in the memories and strength
to embrace each day. Surround me with your
love and guiding light.

**In the tender embrace of grief, we
gather strength for new
beginnings.**

UNDERSTANDING SEASONS OF MOTHERHOOD

"Weeping may endure for a night, but joy comes in the morning."

PSALM 30:5

DEVOTION

Seasons of motherhood will ebb and flow, but remember, each moment is precious and helps shape the incredible journey of both your children and yourself.

REFLECTION

What season of motherhood are you currently experiencing, and how can you embrace its unique beauty and challenges?

____

____

____

____

PRAYER

Dear God, thank You for walking with us through every season of motherhood. Help us to find strength and joy in the ups and downs, nurturing our kids while nurturing ourselves.

Every season of motherhood brings its own set of blessings and lessons; embrace them all.

THE ROLE OF WORSHIP IN FAMILY LIFE

"Serve the Lord with gladness; come before His presence with singing."

PSALM 100:2

DEVOTION

Worship transforms our homes from mere living spaces into places of divine connection, nurturing faith in our families through shared moments of joy and praise.

REFLECTION

What does worship look like in your home, and how can it strengthen your family's bond with each other and with God?

PRAYER

Heavenly Father, bless our homes with Your presence. May our moments of worship together draw us closer to You and to one another, filling our hearts with love and joy.

Worship is the heartbeat of a family; it's where love is nurtured and faith is passed down.

LEARNING FROM JESUS' MOTHER

"I am the Lord's servant," Mary answered. "May your word to me be fulfilled." Then the angel left her.

LUKE 1:38

DEVOTION

In moments of uncertainty or overwhelming responsibility, remember to embrace your own calling with the same grace that Mary showed.

REFLECTION

What qualities do you admire most in Mary, the mother of Jesus, and how can you embody those traits in your own life as a mother and a woman of faith?

____

____

____

____

PRAYER

Dear Lord, thank you for the example of Mary, who showed courage, grace, and unwavering faith. Help me to embrace these qualities in my own journey as a mother and to lean on you as she did.

From her quiet strength to her unwavering faith, Mary teaches us that true devotion shines brightest in the everyday moments of life.

THE POWER OF AFFIRMATION

"Death and life are in the power of the tongue."

PROVERBS 18:21

DEVOTION

Speak life into your soul with intentional affirmations, nurturing a spirit that reflects your strength and resilience.

REFLECTION

What affirmations do you speak over yourself and your children each day, and how do they shape your thoughts and actions? Have you paused to consider the impact of your words on your family's spirit?

____

____

____

____

PRAYER

Dear God, thank you for the gift of words and the power they hold. Help me to speak life, love, and encouragement into my own heart and the hearts of those around me. May my words reflect Your truth and strength.

Your words can either build a fortress of hope or a pit of despair; choose to be the architect of affirmation.

UNDERSTANDING BOUNDARIES

"Let your foot be seldom in your neighbor's house, lest he have his fill of you and hate you."

PROVERBS 25:17

DEVOTION

You are deserving of your own space and priorities; establishing boundaries is a form of self-care that ultimately enriches your relationships.

REFLECTION

What does the word "boundaries" mean to you in your current life, and how can setting healthy boundaries enhance your relationships with your children, partner, and friends?

____

____

____

____

PRAYER

Dear Lord, grant me the wisdom and courage to establish healthy boundaries in my life. Help me to recognize my needs and protect my peace, while also nurturing the connections I hold dear.

Boundaries are not walls; they're gates that help us choose who and what enters our lives.

THE GIFT OF GIVING

"Not looking to your own interests but each of you to the interests of the others."

PHILIPPIANS 2:4

DEVOTION

In the tapestry of life, it is in the moments of giving that we often find our truest purpose and joy.

REFLECTION

What gifts have you been blessed with that you can share with others today? How can you cultivate a spirit of generosity in your daily life?

____

____

____

____

PRAYER

Dear God, thank You for the abundance in our lives. Help me to recognize the needs around me and give me the courage to share my gifts with those who may need them the most.

True generosity is not just in what we give, but in the love behind our giving.

TRANSITIONS IN FAMILY LIFE

"For everything there is a season, and a time for every matter under heaven."

ECCLESIASTES 3:1

DEVOTION

Embrace each transition as a reminder that your family's journey is a series of seasons, each bringing growth and new opportunities for connection and love.

REFLECTION

What transitions are currently taking place in
your family life, and how can you embrace them
with grace and openness?

____

____

____

____

PRAYER

Dear God, help me navigate the changes in my
family with wisdom and love. May Your peace
guide my heart as I embrace each transition,
trusting in Your plan for us.

**Change is not just a phase; it's an
invitation to grow together.**

ADDRESSING FEARS

"I sought the Lord, and he answered me; he delivered me from all my fears."

PSALM 34:4

DEVOTION

Addressing our fears with prayer and faith invites peace and reminds us that even in the quiet, we can find strength in God's presence.

REFLECTION

What fears have been holding you back lately, and how might embracing faith help you to step forward into freedom?

____

____

____

____

PRAYER

Dear God, thank You for always being by my side. Help me to release my fears into Your hands and trust in Your plan for me and my family.

Faith is the bridge between doubt and hope.

ENCOURAGEMENT THROUGH SCRIPTURE

"I lift up my eyes to the hills— where does my help come from? My help comes from the Lord, the Maker of heaven and earth."

PSALM 121:1-2

DEVOTION

When we lift our eyes to God amidst the chaos of life, He will always be our source of help and encouragement.

REFLECTION

What scripture brings you comfort during challenging times, and how can you weave its truths into your daily life as a mother and a woman of faith?

____

____

____

____

PRAYER

Dear Lord, thank You for the gift of Your Word that strengthens and encourages us. Help us to find comfort in scripture today and to share that peace with our loved ones.

Let your heart be anchored in the promises of God, for they are a wellspring of hope and strength.

RESTORING RELATIONSHIPS

"You will keep in perfect peace those whose minds are steadfast, because they trust in you."

ISAIAH 26:3

DEVOTION

The journey to restore relationships often begins with the courage to speak your truth and listen with an open heart.

REFLECTION

What relationships in your life feel strained or broken, and what steps can you take, however small, to begin restoring them today? Consider how reaching out with love and understanding might shift the dynamics you are experiencing.

____

____

____

____

PRAYER

Dear Lord, help me to see the beauty in every relationship and the opportunity for healing. Guide my heart as I seek to mend what is broken, and fill me with patience and grace.

Restoration begins with a single act of kindness.

FINDING YOUR IDENTITY IN CHRIST

"For we are God's masterpiece. He has created us anew in Christ Jesus, so we can do the good things he planned for us long ago."

EPHESIANS 2:10

DEVOTION

Remember that your worth is not tied to your roles or responsibilities; it is rooted in who you are as a beloved daughter of Christ.

REFLECTION

What parts of your life do you struggle to surrender to Christ, and how might letting go of those burdens help you discover your true identity in Him?

____

____

____

____

PRAYER

Heavenly Father, help me to see myself as You see me. Lead me to embrace my identity in Christ, free from the weight of the world's expectations. Fill my heart with peace and purpose as I navigate this journey.

Your true identity is not defined by your role as a mother, wife, or friend, but by the love and grace you receive from Christ.

ACTIVELY SEEKING JOY

"You make known to me the path of life; in your presence there is fullness of joy; at your right hand are pleasures forevermore."

PSALM 16:11

DEVOTION

Seek joy intentionally in the little moments of each day, for that is where happiness often lies waiting for us to discover.

REFLECTION

What small moments of joy have you let slip by recently, and how can you intentionally seek them out today? Consider the unique beauty in your daily routine and how it can bring you happiness.

____

____

____

____

PRAYER

Dear Lord, help me to open my eyes to the joy that surrounds me each day. May I find delight in the ordinary and lift my heart to embrace the moments of gratitude you place in my path. Amen.

Joy is not found in the absence of challenges, but in the presence of gratitude.

THE IMPORTANCE OF LAUGHTER

"Our mouths were filled with laughter, our tongues with songs of joy."

PSALM 126:2

DEVOTION

We must intentionally carve out moments for joy and laughter; they are not just nice additions to our lives but essential for our emotional well-being.

REFLECTION

What brings a genuine smile or a hearty laugh to your day? Can you recall moments of joy that lifted your spirit, even during challenging times?

____

____

____

____

PRAYER

Dear God, thank you for the gift of laughter and the joy it brings into our lives. Help us to embrace moments of lightness and to share that joy with those around us. May we find reasons to laugh every day, even in the ordinary.

Laughter is a gentle reminder that joy can coexist with life's challenges.

CELEBRATING INDIVIDUALITY

"Do not look at his appearance or at his physical stature, because I have refused him. For the Lord does not see as man sees; for man looks at the outward appearance, but the Lord looks at the heart."

1 SAMUEL 16:7

DEVOTION

Embracing your distinct journey can empower you to live authentically and inspire others around you.

REFLECTION

What does being true to yourself look like in your daily life, and how can you embrace the unique gifts that set you apart from others?

____

____

____

____

PRAYER

Dear God, thank you for the beautiful tapestry of individuality you have woven in each of us. Help me to cherish my unique qualities and celebrate the differences in those around me. Amen.

Embrace your uniqueness; it's the key to unlocking your fullest potential.

MANAGING EXPECTATIONS

"In their hearts humans plan their course, but the Lord establishes their steps."

PROVERBS 16:9

DEVOTION

Managing our expectations allows us to pivot gracefully and discover hidden blessings in the unpredictability of life.

REFLECTION

What expectations are you currently placing on yourself as a mother, a partner, or in your personal life, and how do these align with the reality you experience each day?

____

____

____

____

PRAYER

Dear God, help me to release the burdens of unrealistic expectations and embrace the beauty of the present moment. Grant me the wisdom to find joy in the little things and the strength to let go of what I cannot control.

Grace thrives when we let go of perfection.

THE ROLE OF FAITH IN EDUCATION

"I can do all things through Christ who strengthens me."

PHILIPPIANS 4:13

DEVOTION

When we lean on faith, we find not only strength for ourselves but also the ability to empower and inspire our children to persevere in their learning journeys.

REFLECTION

What does faith mean to you in the context of your child's education, and how can you bring that faith into their learning experiences?

____

____

____

____

PRAYER

Dear God, grant me the wisdom to nurture my child's mind and spirit with love and faith. Help me to instill values that encourage not just knowledge, but also a deep trust in Your guidance through their educational journey.

Education is not just about filling the mind; it's about nurturing the heart with faith and purpose.

A Moment of Gratitude

If this devotional has brought moments of peace, strength, or reflection into your life, a short review on Amazon can help others discover it too.

devo.anchoredgraces.com/mother

Even a few words about your experience can make a meaningful difference.

Thank you for continuing this journey.

PATIENCE IN PARENTING

"The Lord is good to those who wait for Him, to the soul who seeks Him. It is good that one should hope and wait quietly for the salvation of the Lord."

LAMENTATIONS 3:25-26

DEVOTION

Cultivating patience in parenting means embracing the messiness of growth—both ours and our children's—while trusting in the timing of God's plan for each moment.

REFLECTION

What are some moments in your parenting journey where you've felt the need to practice patience, and how can you invite God into those moments?

____

____

____

____

PRAYER

Dear Lord, thank you for the gift of motherhood. Grant me the patience to lovingly guide my children, even in the challenging moments, and fill my heart with peace as I trust in Your timing.

Patience is not just waiting; it's how we behave while we wait.

UNDERSTANDING DIFFERENT PARENTING STYLES

"If any of you lacks wisdom, let him ask of God, who gives to all liberally and without reproach, and it will be given to him."

JAMES 1:5

DEVOTION

The most effective parenting style is not about strict adherence to a method, but about being present and responsive to your child's unique needs.

REFLECTION

What are the unique strengths and challenges of your parenting style, and how do they reflect your values and beliefs?

____

____

____

____

PRAYER

Dear God, thank you for the precious gift of our children. Help us to embrace our unique parenting styles and guide us to nurture our children with love and wisdom.

Each parenting style is a beautiful thread in the tapestry of family life.

THE BLESSINGS OF COMMUNITY SERVICE

Carry each other's burdens, and in this way you will fulfill the law of Christ."

GALATIANS 6:2

DEVOTION

Service to others not only blesses those in need but enriches our lives, revealing the beauty of connection and purpose that comes from working together.

REFLECTION

What experiences have you had that made you feel truly connected to your community, and how can you seek out or create more opportunities for service in your life?

____

____

____

____

PRAYER

Dear Lord, thank you for the gift of community and the opportunity to serve. Help me embrace the blessings that come not just from giving, but from the connections and growth that flourish in the hearts of those around me. Amen.

Service to others is the pathway to deep connection and joy.

THE IMPACT OF KINDNESS

"Therefore, as God's chosen people, holy and dearly loved, clothe yourselves with compassion, kindness, humility, gentleness and patience. Bear with each other and forgive one another if any of you has a grievance against someone. Forgive as the Lord forgave you. And over all these virtues put on love, which binds them all together in perfect unity."

COLOSSIANS 3:12-14

DEVOTION

When we choose kindness, we weave connections that uplift not only others but also ourselves, fostering a spirit of community and support.

REFLECTION

What small act of kindness can you extend today that might brighten someone else's day, or even your own? Think about the ripple effects it could create in your family and community.

____

____

____

____

PRAYER

Dear God, thank you for the gift of kindness that you bestow upon us each day. Help us to be vessels of your love and grace, spreading warmth and compassion wherever we go. Amen.

Kindness is the thread that weaves our hearts together, creating a tapestry of love that defines our lives.

FAITH-FILLED LEADERSHIP AT HOME

"Now faith is the assurance of things hoped for, the conviction of things not seen."

HEBREWS 11:1

DEVOTION

Every small act of faith in our homes helps cultivate an environment of trust and love, allowing our children to see God's hand at work through us.

REFLECTION

What does it mean for you to lead your family with faith, and how can you intentionally incorporate your beliefs into your daily interactions with your loved ones?

____

____

____

____

PRAYER

Dear God, thank you for the gift of family and the opportunity to lead with love and faith. Help me to be a beacon of Your wisdom in my home today.

Your leadership at home can plant the seeds of faith that grow into a legacy for generations.

TRUSTING IN GOD'S PROVISION

"I have been young, and now am old; yet I have not seen the righteous forsaken, nor his descendants begging bread."

PSALM 37:25

DEVOTION

God's provision often comes in the most unexpected forms; trust in Him, and you may just find what you need at the perfect moment.

REFLECTION

What worries or needs are currently weighing on your heart, and how can you practice trusting God to provide in those areas? Consider how He has been faithful to you in the past.

____

____

____

____

PRAYER

Dear God, thank you for always being there to meet our needs. Help me to lean into your provision today, trusting that you have a plan for my life and my family.

Trusting in God's provision means letting go of control and believing He knows what is best for us.

THE IMPORTANCE OF RITUALS

"I will remember the deeds of the Lord; yes, I will remember your miracles of long ago. I will meditate on all your works and consider all your mighty deeds."

PSALM 77:11-12

DEVOTION

Creating and maintaining rituals, no matter how small, can help us cultivate a deeper sense of connection and appreciation for the blessings in our lives.

REFLECTION

What rituals do you incorporate into your life that help you feel connected to your family and to yourself? How can you deepen those practices to foster peace and joy in your everyday routine?

____

____

____

____

PRAYER

Dear God, thank you for the gift of routine and ritual in our lives. Help us to embrace the little moments that bring us closer to You and to those we love. May our hearts find peace in the daily rhythms we create.

Rituals are the threads that weave us closer together, creating a tapestry of love and understanding within our families.

EMBRACING DIFFERENCES IN PARENTING

"Every good and perfect gift is from above, coming down from the Father of the heavenly lights, who does not change like shifting shadows."

JAMES 1:17

DEVOTION

Embracing the differences in our children empowers them to flourish into their true selves while reminding us of the beauty in individuality.

REFLECTION

What unique strengths do you bring to your
parenting journey that differ from other
mothers in your life, and how can you celebrate
those distinctions today?

____

____

____

____

PRAYER

Dear God, thank you for the gift of motherhood
and the beautiful differences you have woven
into each of us. Help me to embrace the
uniqueness in my parenting journey and find joy
in the diverse ways we nurture our children.

**Embracing our differences allows
us to create a richer tapestry of
love in our families.**

SAVORING SIMPLE MOMENTS

"Better a small serving of vegetables with love than a fattened calf with hatred."

PROVERBS 15:17

DEVOTION

Sometimes, the most meaningful moments aren't found in grand celebrations but in the quiet dinners at home, where love fills the spaces between us.

REFLECTION

What small, everyday moments have you recently overlooked that might bring you joy if you paused to savor them? How can you cultivate a deeper sense of gratitude for the simple joys in your life?

____

____

____

____

PRAYER

Dear God, thank you for the beauty of everyday moments. Help us to slow down and appreciate the nuances of life and motherhood, finding joy in each precious second. Amen.

Life's sweetest treasures often hide in the ordinary.

CELEBRATING FAMILY TRADITIONS

"All your children shall be taught by the Lord,
and great shall be the peace of your children."

ISAIAH 54:13

DEVOTION

In our busy lives, it's the little traditions that
create lasting bonds, reminding us of our values
and the love that we share as a family.

REFLECTION

What family traditions bring you the deepest joy, and how can you intentionally nurture them in your life and with your loved ones?

____

____

____

____

PRAYER

Dear God, thank you for the gift of family and the joy of our shared traditions. Help us to cherish and cultivate these moments, making memories that will last for generations.

Traditions are the threads that weave our family story together.

FINDING YOUR RHYTHM

"Commit your way to the Lord; trust in Him, and He will act."

PSALM 37:5

DEVOTION

Trusting in God's timing allows us to find our unique rhythm, guiding our hearts through the chaos of life.

REFLECTION

What are the rhythms of your daily life that nurture your spirit and those around you, and which ones feel out of sync?

____

____

____

____

PRAYER

Dear God, help me find peace in my daily rhythm. Guide me to embrace the moments of joy and to navigate the challenges with grace.

Embrace the ebb and flow of your life; each season brings its own melody.

THE POWER OF TOUCH

"Love is patient, love is kind. It does not envy, it does not boast, it is not proud. It does not dishonor others, it is not self-seeking, it is not easily angered, it keeps no record of wrongs. Love does not delight in evil but rejoices with the truth. It always protects, always trusts, always hopes, always perseveres.

1 CORINTHIANS 13:4-7

DEVOTION

In a world often filled with distractions, remember that your touch can convey profound love and understanding, becoming a bridge of connection with those who need you most.

REFLECTION

What are some ways you can intentionally use your touch to convey love and comfort to your family and friends today? How does touching the lives of those around you impact your own heart?

____

____

____

____

PRAYER

Dear Lord, thank you for the gift of touch, which helps us connect deeply with others. May our hands bring comfort and love today, allowing Your warmth to flow through us to those we encounter.

Your embrace can be a healing balm that speaks louder than words.

BUILDING A LEGACY OF FAITH

"We will not hide them from their descendants; we will tell the next generation the praiseworthy deeds of the Lord, his power, and the wonders he has done. He decreed statutes for Jacob and established the law in Israel, which he commanded our ancestors to teach their children, so the next generation would know them."

PSALM 78:4-6

DEVOTION

Our faith is the most precious inheritance we can leave for our children, far surpassing any material wealth.

REFLECTION

What kind of legacy do you want to leave for your children? How are you currently nurturing their faith in everyday moments?

____

____

____

____

PRAYER

Dear Lord, thank You for the gift of motherhood and the opportunity to shape the lives of our children. Help me to be a beacon of faith in my home and to instill Your love in the hearts of my family.

Faith is the silent inheritance we pass down, one prayer and one moment at a time.

THE IMPORTANCE OF BALANCE

"Whatever you do, work at it with all your heart, as working for the Lord, not for human masters, since you know that you will receive an inheritance from the Lord as a reward. It is the Lord Christ you are serving."

COLOSSIANS 3:23-24

DEVOTION

Finding balance in our lives is not just about equal distribution of time; it's about recognizing our needs and valuing our well-being as much as our responsibilities.

REFLECTION

What does balance look like in your life right now, and how can you nurture that sense of equilibrium amidst your many responsibilities?

____

____

____

____

PRAYER

Dear God, help me find balance in the chaos of daily life. Grant me the wisdom to prioritize my time and the strength to embrace my journey with grace.

Balance is not something you find; it's something you create.

EMBRACING VULNERABILITY

"Blessed are those who mourn, for they will be comforted."

MATTHEW 5:4

DEVOTION

Vulnerability is not a sign of weakness but a pathway for deeper connection and grace in our lives.

REFLECTION

What does it mean for you to embrace vulnerability in your life, and how might it deepen your connections with those you love?

____

____

____

____

PRAYER

Dear God, help me to see my vulnerability as a source of strength, not weakness. May I find the courage to be open and honest with myself and those around me, allowing Your love to flow into my life and relationships.

True strength lies not in the absence of fear, but in our willingness to be open despite it.

Near the End of Our Journey

You have spent many days reflecting through these devotionals.

If this book has supported your spiritual journey, sharing a short review on Amazon helps more women discover these pages of encouragement.

devo.anchoredgraces.com/mother

Your story may be the reason another woman finds hope.

EMBRACING STRENGTH IN EVERY SEASON

"The name of the Lord is a strong tower; the righteous man runs into it and is safe."

PROVERBS 18:10

DEVOTION

Allow yourself to lean into your faith, recognizing that true strength is found in surrendering your worries to God, who embraces you in every season of your life.

REFLECTION

What does strength mean to you in this season of your life, and how can you embrace it in your daily routines?

____

____

____

____

PRAYER

Dear God, thank you for the strength you provide in every season of our lives. Help us to embrace our unique journeys, finding comfort and courage in your unwavering presence. May we always remember that we are never alone in our struggles.

True strength is not the absence of struggle, but the grace to rise with resilience after each fall.

THE ART OF COMPROMISE

"Bear with each other and forgive one another if any of you has a grievance against someone. Forgive as the Lord forgave you."

COLOSSIANS 3:13

DEVOTION

In every relationship, even in the midst of disagreement, there lies a chance for connection through the art of compromise.

REFLECTION

What areas in your life are you holding on to too tightly, and how might a spirit of compromise bring you greater peace and joy in your relationships? Consider how letting go could bless not just you, but your loved ones as well.

____

____

____

____

PRAYER

Dear God, help me to see the beauty in compromise. May I find strength and grace in the moments of giving and taking, so that I may nurture deeper connections with those I love. Amen.

True strength lies not in holding our ground, but in the gentle art of meeting others halfway.

STRENGTHENING MARITAL BONDS

"Let all that you do be done in love."

1 CORINTHIANS 16:14

DEVOTION

In the ebb and flow of life's responsibilities, remember that small acts of love can build a fortress around your relationship, making it resilient against the storms of everyday life.

REFLECTION

What are some small, intentional ways you can show your partner love and appreciation this week? Reflect on how these gestures can strengthen your marital bond.

____

____

____

____

PRAYER

Dear God, help us to nurture our marriages with love and kindness. May our hearts be open to understanding, and our actions reflect the commitment we make to one another.

Love is not just a feeling; it is the daily choice to uplift and cherish your partner.

AMPLIFYING CHILDREN'S VOICES

"...so that you may become blameless and pure, "children of God without fault in a warped and crooked generation." Then you will shine among them like stars in the sky 16 as you hold firmly to the word of life. And then I will be able to boast on the day of Christ that I did not run or labor in vain."

PHILIPPIANS 2:15-16

DEVOTION

To amplify our children's voices, we must listen deeply, allowing their words to flourish in our presence.

REFLECTION

What are some ways you can create space in your day to hear your child's thoughts and feelings more deeply?

____

____

____

____

PRAYER

Dear God, thank You for the gift of our children and the unique voices they bring into our lives. Help us to listen with open hearts and nurture their thoughts, allowing them to feel valued and understood.

Every voice deserves to be heard, especially those of our children; they often carry wisdom we are yet to discover.

PRACTICING FORGIVENESS DAILY

"For if you forgive other people when they sin against you, your heavenly Father will also forgive you. But if you do not forgive others their sins, your Father will not forgive your sins."

MATTHEW 6:14-15

DEVOTION

Forgiveness is a daily choice that frees our hearts and opens the door to renewed relationships and inner peace.

REFLECTION

What situations in your life are you holding onto that could benefit from the gentle act of forgiveness? How might releasing these burdens foster peace in your heart and strengthen your relationships?

____

____

____

____

PRAYER

Dear God, guide me in my journey of forgiveness. Help me to release the weight of past hurts and embrace the freedom that comes with letting go. Fill my heart with your love and compassion, so I may also share these gifts with others.

Forgiveness is not just a gift to others; it is a grace to ourselves.

More Devotionals from Anchored Grace

If this devotional encouraged your heart, you may also enjoy these devotionals from Anchored Grace.

- 365 Day Devotional for Women
- 90 Day Devotional for Women Seeking Peace
- 90 Day Devotional for Women Facing Anxiety and Stress
- 90 Day Devotional for Women 50+
- Guided Prayer Journal for Women

Search **"Anchored Grace Devotional"** on Amazon to discover more devotionals designed to support your journey of faith.

Thank you for spending this devotional journey with Anchored Grace.

If this devotional encouraged your heart, strengthened your faith, or brought peace to your daily routine, would you consider leaving a short review on Amazon?

devo.anchoredgraces.com/mother

Reviews help other women discover devotionals that may support them through their own seasons of life.

Even a single sentence about your experience can make a difference.

We are grateful you chose Anchored Grace.